# Illuminated Manuscript

# ILLUMINATED MANUSCRIPT

David Schelhaas

Dordt College Press

Cover design: Robert Haan
Cover photo: Calvin Jongsma
Layout: Carla Goslinga

© 2012 David Schelhaas

Fragmentary portions of this book may be freely used by those who are interested in sharing this author's insights and musings, so long as the material is not pirated for monetary gain and so long as proper credit is visibly given to the publisher and the author. Others, and those who wish to use larger sections of text, must seek written permission from the publisher.

*Printed in the United States of America.*

Dordt College Press  www.dordt.edu/dordt_press
498 Fourth Avenue NE
Sioux Center, Iowa 51250
United States of America

ISBN-13: 978-0-932914-95-8

Library of Congress Control Number: 2012943087

*Nature is a shining garment in which
God is revealed and concealed.*

—John Calvin as paraphrased by Marilynne Robinson—

## Dedication

To our grandchildren,
Paige, Carter, Taryn, Corrie, and Nico.

You are all children of light.

# Contents

## Illuminated Manuscript
Illuminated Manuscript ................................................................. 1
And God Said Softly, "Music" ...................................................... 2
On Planning a Poetry Class Schedule for
    the Last Third of the Semester .................................................. 4
Leaves in the Wind ........................................................................ 5
Doubt Denied ................................................................................. 6
I Attempt to Explain the Incarnation ........................................... 7
The Turning of Her Head .............................................................. 8
Definitions of Hang Time .............................................................. 9
Steps in the Sacrament of Sequoia Viewing ............................. 10
In Bandon, Oregon ...................................................................... 11
His Holy Temples ......................................................................... 12
Milkweed Pod .............................................................................. 13
Upon Learning that April is Genocide Prevention Month ........ 14

## The Old Professor and Others
The Old Professor Ruminates On Vanity ................................. 17
My Father Counting, Singing ..................................................... 19
What Gentled You? ..................................................................... 20
Bad Guys ...................................................................................... 21
The Teacher .................................................................................. 22
Uncle Jack Washes Up for Dinner ............................................. 23
Smoking with Jimmy B ............................................................... 24
Tena, Tena, Sour and Crabby ..................................................... 26
The Old Professor Ponders Laughter ........................................ 28
Cricket Ball ................................................................................... 31
Hair, 1956 ..................................................................................... 32
The Old Professor Discovers the Sweet Egg of Discontent ..... 33

## Already and Not Yet
Already and Not Yet .................................................................... 37
The Proper Way to Paint a Winter Morning ............................. 38
The Trees this Morning ............................................................... 39
Warm and Sunny ......................................................................... 40

| | |
|---|---|
| Nine Lines | 41 |
| Mixed Messages | 42 |
| A Grain of Seed Must Die | 43 |
| Return | 44 |
| Retired | 45 |
| Single-Heartedness | 46 |
| After the Harvest | 47 |
| Winter | 48 |

# Illuminated Manuscript

# Illuminated Manuscript

> OUR LORD REIGNS
> BANANAS—2# FOR 59
> FLOWERS
> *(Seen on a lighted rent-a-sign at a fruit market in Muskegon, Michigan)*

During a spring snowstorm
I saw the sign and dismissed it,
April snowstorms being conducive to doubt.

But a brief flurry of crocuses two weeks later
chipped away at my wintry agnosticism.
And then one day on the road to work
I was nearly blinded by daffodil and forsythia shine.

After that, doubt didn't stand a chance.
Petunias, tulips, impatiens pattered down,
catching in window boxes, along sidewalks.
Rhododendrons thundered from lavender clouds,
dandelions crackled in jagged lines across green lawns.

Oh, yes!
Our Lord reigns,
Rains flowers.

Fruit showers,
forecast for later in the summer,
came as predicted.

Strawberries and raspberries gushed through gutters,
a Red Sea miracle.
Plums the size of golf balls pelted unprotected cars.
Bananas whirling like boomerangs filled the air.
Apples, peaches, pears came down like cats and dogs,
all together,
all singing a rainbow promise:
Our Lord Reigns!

# AND GOD SAID SOFTLY, "MUSIC"

It must have been early in the morning of the fourth day
that God in the pre-dawn, deep-blue-blackness whispered to himself,
"Music,"
though it wasn't the English word, *music,*
English not yet existing, nor for that matter any other earth
language. God said "Music" softly in God language,
as he imagined all those birds at dawn —
though why it had to be birds that sang and not, say,
rodents or cats or large non-human mammals — I don't know.
(Blue whales, of course, sing and have actually made a best-selling album,
still it's birds that are the earth's primary singers —
they do it for a living, so to speak.)
But he must have heard in his mind's ear
all those birds waking up, breaking the silence
with their first hesitant chirps and cheeps, trills and gurgles,
then gradually gaining confidence and soaring into songs of dawn.

What a good idea, music, maybe his best creation
though it's hard to pick one best thing,
humans being a pretty good idea, in spite of the fall,
and marriage and sex, and all the tasty foods,
and language, all languages,
but especially English — and here I know my bias is showing —
English being my native language and the only one I speak.

But back to music. I suspect it was birds who planted
in humans the notion that they could sing,
and then pretty soon Jubal was tinkering with strings and whistles
and not long after that in God time, I stood in the Chorus
of The Siouxland Oratorio singing with others
the great choruses of Handel's *Messiah*. He
knew what he was doing — I mean God, not Handel — though Handel
certainly did all right and so did the Chorus and Orchestra —
but we're all just birds, really, all of us warbling
as best we can in praise of the Creator, who back in the darkness
of pre-creation thought how nice it would be to hear his creation sing.
And perhaps he also thought then how much his creatures
might be comforted by the songs they sang to him.

I'll bet he did.

# On Planning a Poetry Class Schedule for the Last Third of the Semester

I'm in my office on this bright, windy March day,
but my eyes keep glancing out my window at the shadows
of the giant maple that are waving at me, pulling my heart toward
my yard, littered with the debris of winter,
and my garden where the soil needs to be tilled
for lettuce and radishes and peas. I am caught
in the age-old tension between pleasure and duty.

Let's see, what should we do
on the week you get back from spring break?
We could spend a day talking about "turning the line" and enjambment,
but what if the wind is coming out of the North at gale force that day?
Shouldn't we all march outside, stick our heads into the wind and
walk a fresh-plowed field due north till it turns us back toward home?
And if on the same day that you are scheduled to read
your sonnets aloud in class,
the air is so sweet
you think you're sipping honeysuckle when you breathe
and so soft
you want to caress it before you inhale it,
should we be sitting stiff in our gleaming Formica desks,
our ears alert for broken meter or false rhyme?

The rest of the school year sits before us like a haiku
— seventeen days like seventeen syllables,
each one vital but each one subject to shifts and changes
at an instant's notice as we play with the materials at hand.
So let it be a liquid haiku that we make of these last seventeen days.
And may five of those syllables be these oldest, dearest friends of
poets everywhere:

May we rub our hands and arms
across the deep grooved bark of old cottonwoods,
savor the green juices of newborn grasses,
listen to the wind fretting last fall's cattails,
inhale the odor of red maple buds as we walk across parking lots,
catch each darting shaft of gold as finches paint the sky,

and may our eyes gush tears from spring's brisk winds
as we grieve for all the signs of new life that go unsensed,
the wind telling the sweet old saga of freshly turned soil,
the creek singing the minnow's silver scales.

# Leaves in the Wind

Dark linden leaves flutter on the umber couch in my study,
shadows cast by the morning sun. Sunbeams draw my eyes
outward to the tree where only a few leaves still hang
and into the blue sky beyond, where God sits, somewhere,
laughing, perhaps, or puzzled,
as he deals out rain and wind and snow
around the globe. Here, he's spreading out buttery sunshine—
and leaves, of course, which are raining down everywhere after last night's frost.
Weather, war, the starving hoards—he must
get tired of deciding things.
And all those prayers that fly at him like leaves in the wind,
words, words, words in a thousand different languages,
some confident and faith full,
some doubt full and timid as shy boys at a dance.
How does he do it?
Does he grab one here and there
to answer and let the rest float on by?
Oh, I know what the Book says but
it is not always enough.
The evidence of things seen
beggars glib conclusion.

Do you think you know God? That you can
go after him like a big game hunter, net him with
large Latin words—omnipotent, omnipresent, omniscient—
and cage him in a catechism?

I sit here all day fiddling with words,
trying to put them into some sort of tune,
an arrangement that harmonizes God,
the world and my question-cluttered mind.
Better to go outside and rake
my leaf-littered lawn.

## Doubt Denied

The door to doubt need not be opened wide,
A finger's breadth of space will quite suffice
For numbing winds to silently invade
The lungs and turn the soul to ice.
Nor need the door be opened very long
For that old merchant doubt to hustle through
And sing his mercenary peddler's song:
"Come buy, come buy, hard questions just for you."
Faith reels and totters, grasps at certainties
That can't sustain because faith at its core
Resides in unseen depth of mystery.
But then a shaft of song shoots through the door:
A wren who can't but sing her maker's praise
Has pierced cold doubt and set cold faith ablaze.

# I Attempt to Explain the Incarnation

How ever it happened —
and it defies all knowing —
God who is Spirit
planted a physical seed
in the womb of a flesh and blood woman,
a seed that contained the essence of the Son
who had been of one substance with the Father from all time,
but would now be of a different substance,
though not a created substance,
for he was begotten, not made.
> Where this unmade seed came from,
> how it joined with the ovum of woman to become Jesus,
> what happened to the Son who had been co-eternal
> with the Father and the Spirit
> once the flesh and blood fetus began to grow
> in the womb of the woman,
> and how he was from that moment of planting
> no longer simply spirit
> but flesh and blood and bone,
> this is deepest mystery.

And this is mystery just as deep:
Once committed to physicality,
Jesus never looked back
but took on flesh for eternity.
> His was not a thirty-three year gig on the Earth branch
> of the Creation Corporation
> with guarantee he'd be transferred back to heaven
> to don again airy spirituality
> after discarding all that cumbersome flesh and blood and bone.

When God in Christ took on flesh, he took it on for good,
bound himself to humanity forever.
Right now Jesus sits in a real body at the metaphorical right hand of God the Father.
> Do you find this hard? It *is* hard! That Christ,
> having put on this ungodly flesh,
> has chosen to retain it, eschewing perfect likeness
> with the Father and Spirit for continuing corporality —
> as if the human body, now incorruptible, was something desirable.

Oh, joyful materiality!
Praise God from whom all bodies flow.

# The Turning of Her Head (A Found poem)*

She is gone.
More like she is on a journey
and we are to follow soon.
Often when we are praying by the table
at meal times, eyes closed,
I visualize her sitting next to me.
We miss her yet have joy in our hearts
knowing she is in the great white throng
singing the song of Salvation with palm
in her hand and the crown of righteous
glory on her head.
Wonderful!

No time there,
No today, yesterday
or tomorrow
for her.
The turning of her head
and we will all be there.

What Glory!

*The opening lines of a letter written by Albert Schelhaas (my dad) to his daughter Judy shortly after the death of his wife.*

# Definitions of Hang Time

**hang time** n. 1 the length of time a punt hangs
in the sky between kick and catch  2  Michael
Jordan waiting in the air above the hardwood
until his opponents, pulled down by gravity and
a sense of inadequacy, leave an open path for
his feathery shot  3  the five seconds of gorgeous billowing
sound that bounces around the vast gothic vaults
of York Minster after the choir has stopped sing-
ing  4  the loneliest man nailed between earth and
sky as all past, present, and future sins drawn like
iron filings to his immense magnetic heart stop oh
most precious life from pulsing through his veins

## Steps in the Sacrament of Sequoia Viewing

"Be Still" when first you see them.
(You don't really have to be
told this, for silence will be your
natural response.)

"Remember" that some were here
before Christ was born.

"Laugh and Dance" for soon
a bubble of merriment will fill
your soul, a smile expand your face
and, perhaps, a slow swaying movement
will take over your body
in rhythm with the movement of the leaves.

"Babble" if you must, you will not be alone.
The gibberish you hear coming out of your mouth
is known as High Sierra Sequoia glossolalia.

"Touch" but don't bother trying to hug a Sequoia,
even if you feel a surge of love in its presence.
They are too large to hug.

"Clap your hands" and perhaps
all the trees of the field will join your applause
for the Maker of Heaven and Earth.

## In Bandon, Oregon

After a day of driving along the Pacific coast
stopping at one scenic vista after another,
we had gone to the beach for a walk,
some exercise after a day in the car.
Other couples like us, older, holding hands,
dreamy in the haze of a world filled with so much beauty,
were waiting for the sunset to put an exclamation point on the day.

On the horizon two young men in wetsuits,
black silhouettes against the setting sun,
struggled with their surfboards as they
tried to coax a modest wave into a ride.
Occasionally they managed to stay up for several seconds
before losing the wave and disappearing.

Then we saw two others, their heads black
against the lowering sun. Not boys
on surfboards but seals bodysurfing.
We watched them throw their sleek black bodies
sideways into a wave, ride it toward the shore
then quickly swim back out.

Boys and seals,
four black dots against the reddening sky,
rode in, swam out,
in and out,
boys and seals
moving like the words of a poem
written diagonally across a sheet of sea paper
lined with white waves,
till the sun fell behind the water
and the surfers dissolved into the dusky night,
a poem written in water.

## His Holy Temples

All semester they drifted
in and out of lectures and discussions,
sleeping, dreaming, scoring
last minute touchdowns,
hypnotized by golden calves
or marbled biceps.
But now they are madly writing,
their mouths pulled taut, minds moving like lightning,
their pens more slowly than their minds —
back and forth, back and forth across the bluebook page.
They have never been more focused
in their lives. They stare at their papers,
at the ceiling, scratch noses and ears,
blow on fingers, cough and sniff and sniff.
No one smiles.
Dressed in ragged blue-jeans, they scratch
their scraggly beards, smooth their shower-wet hair.
"Beautiful," I think as I watch them, "they are so beautiful,
in this moment, so full of hope, so pure in heart."
I want to tell them
"You will never be more alive
than you are right now,"
tell them, "this attempt to make
from the stuff of your mind
a hard, clear prose that shines and illumines
like the ice on the branches outside the window,
this very action — not the grade you get
or the career you some day find — but this
order that you bring from roiling chaos,
this creation, is the purpose of your
education."
But I merely fold my hands and whisper,
"The Lord is in his Holy Temple,
Let all the Earth keep silence before him."

# Milkweed Pod

Peanut-shaped package,
pale green Christmas tree bulb,
oversized bullet in a velvet casing — lovely
milkweed pod, I run my thumbnail from tip
to stem and open a wonder —
hundreds of dark brown seeds woven together
into a single cone, like freshly stained wood shingles
on the steeple of an old Lutheran church,
each seed tiny as an infant's fingernail,
each attached to white gossamer
more delicate than a newborn's hair.

On my desk two days later, the seeds
in the still tender pod have puffed themselves out
like an aroused hedgehog
and by week's end they've stretched so far forward,
the slightest movement of my body,
the flex of a finger,
sends winged seeds floating round the room.

With casket of milkweed seed in hand
I return to its Sandy Hollow prairie home
and watch the tiny seeds trust themselves
to the wind, flutter
like butterflies upon the breeze
hoping to catch
safely in a bed of soil.
Most will fail.

The several hundred
milkweed pods in this small patch
of prairie will soon crack and dispatch
their seeds to no applause, no human exclamation
of amazement, little chance of success,
each pod a small church sending forth
into the world apostles of beauty.

Like missionaries they go, certain of their calling,
trusting that the gentle breath of the spirit
will bring them safely to their new home.

# Upon Learning that April Is Genocide Prevention Month

As if April didn't have enough to do,
here she comes babbling about genocide prevention.

Sweet, hippie-girl April, with her daffodils everywhere
shouting their happy yellow song and waving at me as I pass,
April, with grass so green it hurts my eyes,
and young trees dressed in thin green-gold ingénue frocks,
bright and fragile and hopeful,
ready to dance the night away at the prom.

What would you have us do?
Shall we send a flower to a warlord?
A bouquet of daisies
to a mother as she spreads thin sand
over slaughtered sons and daughters?
Sweet, foolish, flower-garlanded April,
do you think that a few choruses of
"Give peace a chance" will do the trick?

What is Darfur to you, dear April? Death in The Congo?
Those boys holding big guns in their small hands,
will you invite them to the prom?

Fair April, come away with me
to beautiful, downtown Gaza,
to the Sudan sands where we'll catch the perfect tan,
to the Congo's lush jungles, ever green.
We will weave garlands of bones to wear round our necks
and dance the genocide prevention dance,
our hands stretched upward, eyes wide,
mouths shouting soundlessly,
"No!"

It won't change anything, April,
but at least next year, when you're
asked to be Genocide Prevention month, you can say,
"Thanks, but I did that last year."

# The Old Professor and Others

# The Old Professor Ruminates on Vanity

On his morning walk down Fourth Avenue,
he saw a burr oak about the size that his was now,
well, not his, really, but the college's — yet given
to the college in honor of his retirement
by the Justice Club which he had sponsored for so many years.
He had been pleased by the choice of burr oak,
sturdy old citizen of the mostly treeless prairie,
a survivor like the children of early settlers
who still farmed their little bottom farms,
tough and feisty and stubborn,
an oak like the one his old neighbor Wilbur planted twenty years ago —
a two foot twig stuck in the soil and circled by a Folgers can —
now having twisted and turned its way to a height of fifteen feet,
with branches that stuttered, stopped and started again,
full of passion and indecision.
"A bit like me," the old professor smiled,
straightening his back so he would not look old
as he ascended a rise in the path. He had been thinking
it should have a small plaque at its base with his name on it,
and though he sensed that smacked of vanity,
he'd always held vanity to be a humble fault.
He chuckled at the linking of *fault* and *humble*, mumbling
as he passed Faith Church, "To want to be remembered
after you're gone cannot be wrong, and after all
it's not a dormitory or a Chair I want my name on
but a plaque beneath a tree where perhaps
some grad a decade hence may pass
and seeing it, smile and softly say, 'Ah, the old professor,'
and remember a line from one of the poets,
Hopkins or Dickinson perhaps."
Here the old Professor paused for a moment and then,
his pace quickening and his eyes bright, as if he had received a vision,
said, "They all put their names beneath their poems."

He walked with that a while but could not let it rest,
knowing the tree was not something he had made,
like a poem. But suppose the plaque said,
"Burr Oak, made by God and given to the college

by the Justice Club upon the retirement of Professor . . . ."
On First Avenue he turned as if by instinct
so he could walk past Wilbur's oak,
the Folgers can at its base long since rusted away.
The oak looked fine in the late fall sunrise, a few umber leaves
still fluttering in the breeze, hanging on, "selving" Hopkins might say,
"flinging out their name." He stopped and then as
as if to plant the idea more firmly in his mind, repeated,
"To want to be remembered after you're gone cannot be wrong."

But the Old Professor had never been able to look at a tree
or an idea from just one side and now he stopped
and thought, "How petty this angling for love and remembrance,
and vain as well in the way of the Old Preacher of Ecclesiastes."
He chewed on this as he stood beneath Wilbur's oak,
a tough muscular bantamweight of a tree where
a brassy red squirrel was now skittering from limb to limb,
chattering in double forte, and he thought of Dickinson
refusing to tell her name like a frog to the admiring bog.
"How petty this angling for love and remembrance," he said again,
then turned abruptly and headed for home, his mind made up:
The tree was all he needed and much more
than he had expected. And anyway, as another poet said,
"To live in mankind is far more than to live in a name."

He ascended the steps to his front door,
and then, noting the lovely family nameplate his wife had bought
years ago in Europe and affixed beside the doorjamb,
he sighed once more and mumbled,
"Still, a plaque is a lovely way to . . . ."

# My Father Counting, Singing (A Pantun)

Happy-go-lucky is what the townsfolk called him,
I saw his darker, pensive side sometimes.
The Minnesota sun shines on the coldest days —
My father covered trouble with a whistle or a song.

I saw his darker, pensive side sometimes,
I watched him counting money at the till.
My father covered trouble with a whistle or a song,
The old song and dance that got him through the war.

I watched him counting money at the till
In the evening as we put the store to bed.
The old song and dance that got him through the war —
Was the music he made lament or lullaby?

In the evening as we put the store to bed,
The coins clinking in the tray could cast a spell.
Was the music he made lament or lullaby?
Fifty years have passed since we two closed the store.

The coins clinking in the tray could cast a spell,
A metronome that measured out the years.
Fifty years have passed since we two closed the store.
The heart can grow a callous over time.

A metronome that measured out the years —
My father counting coins and singing in the store.
The heart can grow a callous over time,
But I recall the sadness of twilight's dying glow.

My father counting coins and singing in the store,
Happy-go-lucky is what the townsfolk called him,
But I recall the sadness of twilight's dying glow.
The Minnesota sun shines on the coldest days.

## What Gentled You?

I remember how you shook your head
as we drove by pens of fattening cattle,
a thousand or more packed together knee-deep in muck.
"No way to treat an animal," you fumed.

And I have seen your face light up
when our old cat chooses your old lap
from all those spread around the room
and purrs some secret only you can hear.

Farther back I see you
in your working days on the windswept farm
each autumn butchering hogs and steers. Rabbits
you have shot hang stripped and gutted,
frozen kewpie dolls along the attic rafters.
And I wonder what gentled you that you
became the lover of all helpless living things.

Last Saturday as I trimmed the lower branches of the maple,
you stood by leaning on your cane, heard me exclaim
how glad I was to have those limbs removed,
and answered back, "How do you think the tree feels?"

"What do *you* know of trees and steers and cats?"
I want to ask.
Instead I'll wait and see if I can learn
by watching as you watch the fox kits
frolic in your yard, step so as to miss the crickets
in the stairwell of the cellar, and listen to
the trees, the leafless trees
crying in the wind.

## Bad Guys

In your large crabapple tree
we galloped though long summer afternoons
riding its arching, diving branches like broncos,
the bark smoothed by countless denimed seats.
We were the good guys *and* the bad guys
firing crabapple bullets
at each other till we dropped,
dying slow dramatic deaths
as we swung toward the earth.

After the cancer got into your brain
we never rode again
nor did I come to see you, dying,
so frightened was I by bad guys
I couldn't see.

# The Teacher

Against the darkening October sky,
he walks, briefcase in hand,
shoulders bent down and slightly forward,
eyes turned so deep within himself
they do not see streetlights, dancing tree shadows,
or the low October moon just above the tree line,
but are eyes illuminated instead by brighter visions inside his head —
a boy happily lost in Middle Earth,
another who does complicated long division problems for fun,
a girl whose study of the Ogallala aquifer
has tapped a steady flow of water poems —
the whole fertile bunch of them,
asking and arguing, pulled by the tide
of a new idea, excited, curious, alive.

He is asking himself how he can revive
that moment, rekindle the brush fire that
crackled across his room today.
He is beyond my reach as he goes past
my house not ten yards away,
his mind held captive
by the play
of tomorrow's possibilities.

# Uncle Jack Washes Up for Dinner

Dark with dust from making hay,
he stands at the old porch sink
working the small pump handle.
His face wears a grin the size of a dinner plate,
the smile wrinkling out all the way to his ears
like dark parentheses. The boys sit
on the other end of the porch, arguing and playing jackknife
over a splintery piece of pine. I am the homesick town-cousin
in the middle.

He rubs a rough gray bar of Lava in his hands,
makes suds, then works it into his face, soap-water dripping down
his arms and neck, hands moving hard
back and forth and round and round,
following the laugh lines into eye sockets and ears,
fingers squishing through the ear furrows,
all the while talking through the soap bubbles,
asking in his teasing voice if I brought my appetite along from town,
saying what a fine job I did carrying the bundles to the shockers.
His hands under the spout of the small porch pump,
he bends his head to douse his face,
snorting and snuffling underneath the splash,
washing soap scum from his skin and
childish fears from my faint heart.

## Smoking with Jimmy B

How you hated books
when you were my student,
stabbing and gouging your lit book
front cover to back so that
by year's end it looked as though
someone had blasted it with a shotgun.

I worried that your hatred
carried over to me, but when I gave
you a bit part in a play I directed,
you claimed me as friend.

After graduation—though
you never got a diploma—you
would occasionally appear outside
my classroom when the last bell had rung,
a pack of Winstons wound into the sleeve
of your sweat-stained T-shirt,
and in your loud monotone voice
ask, "Wanna smoke?"

You were a sly one, Jimmy,
luring me from my work with guilt and cigarettes.
You'd shake one out for me, one for yourself,
and we'd stand by the open window in my classroom
smoking and talking: "The guys are going to get beat
tonight," I'd say, and you, having learned this trick
of conversation, would rephrase my words,
"So you think they're gonna get their asses kicked, huh?"
laughing and loving the naughtiness of *asses*.

Now you're gone, snatched early from the sort of life
you'd managed to construct. The news of your death
brings back your eager grin and proffered cigarettes.
Like sad dreams, they hang in my mind,
and I want to say "so long."

Maybe I'll walk down to the Art Department

and bum a smoke from the one guy I know
who still smokes, light up, and say,
"Here's to my former student Jimmy B
who taught me more than I did him."
We'll stand there in his studio and watch the smoke
curl off our cigarettes and out the window,
floating like incense before the mercy-seat of God.

# Tena, Tena, Sour and Crabby

Judy and I watched her all through our childhood
In her long black dress, bent over,
Stabbing dandelions with a butcher knife,
Tending rutabagas in her garden,
Sidling through our father's store,
A scratchy "hello" the only word she ever spoke
To the clerk who took her money.

Her face was sour and wrinkled and turned in on itself
Like an old potato left in the garden all winter long.

When we sulked and pouted in our little house,
Our mother stopped our frowns
By saying, "If you don't watch out,
You'll grow up to be like Tena Goens,"
Which meant to us, alone and mean and
Poor and sour and crabby.

Her hair was gray and yellow, like the rutabagas
Caked with dirt, lying on her stoop.

In my teens I delivered groceries to her house,
Still leery. My heart stopped one afternoon
When a sparrow shot from a downspout by her door
And nearly hit me in the eye. Another time
She took two pennies from her mouth to go
With three I'd given in change to make a nickel,
Wet pennies from her sticky sour mouth.
I dropped them in the grass outside the door.

Her eyes, old copper pennies, were rheumy,
Dull and brown.

Ah, Tena, wrinkled, scowling, slanting down the street
Toward your bleak brown house,
I know now
The whole world is twisted, gnarled, slant, sidewinding,
Crooked, cross and crabbed.

Except where the world's true light
Shines to make a life that's lovely and that loves.

Her life was dark yet no one lit a candle in
Her bleak brown house.

# THE OLD PROFESSOR PONDERS LAUGHTER

He was remembering a time he had seen
an elderly man and wife walking down Main Street—
just past the doctor's office—she'd given
her man a gentle elbow in the ribs
and then they threw back their heads,
laughing to high heaven. He did not know why
they were laughing, but he could see they were sharing
a joy so intimate and private that, watching them
out there on Main Street, he felt like a voyeur.
He had often felt the gentle elbow of his wife and
whooped in laughter at her words as they walked
arm and arm. Shared laughter, he knew, between
a husband and a wife, could be intimate as sex.

His life had been rich with joy,
and he'd had his share of laughter,
(he knew, of course, that these two need not dwell together)
but still he wished he had laughed more,
for fun, but also as a way to shake his fist
at the troubles of the world and say,
"Deep joy will triumph in the end."

There had always been laughter in his classroom,
though it had usually surprised him when it came—
he was not one to tell jokes or build funny moments
into his lectures. Usually it happened
when he was responding spontaneously to something
the class had read or a student had said,
an accidental pun or scatological slip of the tongue.
But the momentary laughter and happiness
that tittered round the room was a beautiful thing,
he thought, something to value for its own sake.

Yesterday he had listened to his grandchildren
playing in the next room, talking and laughing,
their words and giggles (lovely word) punctuated
with shouts and shrieks, and it all seemed
to bubble up as easily and naturally as breath.

Adults, at least the adults he knew,
rarely laughed that way.

He remembered how as a child he had loved to be tickled
yet had fought against it, sensing that
laughter could contain something dangerous,
a kind of fearful helplessness, loss of control,
that put thoughts of death in his mind.
It had been years since he had been tickled,
but he did not think he missed it.

He recalled with pleasure the wonderful helplessness
of trying to hold back laughter at catechism or family devotions
as one of his cousins would pull a face or make an obscene gesture—
how he would duck and cover his mouth and hold his breath
but how in the end the laugh would win,
explode like a fart, and he would sit red-faced and penitent,
waiting for punishment or grace.
And then much later, with his own children—
and even his wife—laughing at table devotions,
how he had wanted to join them but felt obligated
to play the stern father role. He should have
laughed with them. (But if he had,
would it have spoiled the fun?)

One could try to describe the physiology of a laugh—
a vocal burst, explosion of air from the lungs,
watering eyes, breathlessness, loss of strength,
the inability to talk. Both of his daughters—now grown—
still surrender so totally to laughter that they become
helpless. He loved to see them joyfully
wrapped in laughter's soft-muscled arms.

Refreshing, enigmatic, sometimes sinister, amazing—
he could not imagine life without laughter.
But why, he wondered, did Holy Scripture have
so little laughter in it and speak so rarely of it.
Abraham and Sarah laugh, but laugh in disbelief.

God sits in the heavens and laughs in scorn at the wicked,
but does God never chortle in sheer joy at the marvels of his handiwork?
We read "Jesus wept" but never "Jesus laughed"
though he must have laughed some when he was telling his stories.
A man with a log in his eye? And Peter, full of bluster and
cocky as a rooster? Perhaps, the old professor thought,
the gospel writers took themselves too seriously. After all
the catechism says that except for sin Jesus was like us,
so he must have laughed.

He thought of Psalm 126, where the Lord restores
the fortunes of Zion, and people's mouths are filled with laughter,
and their tongues with songs of joy — surely
the sweetest tasting text in all of scripture — reminding us that
only laughter and song are ample enough
to express our greatest joys.

But still remained the riddle of the absence
of a Jesus laugh in sacred writ,
and the old professor chewed on that
like a horse will struggle with a bit
till one day he read what G. K. Chesterton had said:
"There was some one thing that was too great
for God to show us when he walked upon our earth;
and I have sometimes fancied that it was his mirth."

Yes, too great, he thought, but also too sublime
for God to show to creatures bound by time.

# CRICKET BALL

This red, scuffed globe,
stitched with six white lines of
thread running parallel,
three above
three below
the equator-like crack at the center
where the hemispheres of leather meet,
was a gift from my son
who fished it from
a river in Oxford.

My wife and I sat on the bank
and watched young Englishmen
in white slacks and sweaters
play cricket on a field of greenest green
while our children punted on the River Cherell.

Six of us had crossed an ocean
for moments like this,
each of us a separate line of thread
running its course,
now held close together
by this journey, this moment,
and the gravity of love.

# Hair, 1956

We were all in love
with our hair in those days
and so we let it grow
and oiled it up till we could slick
it to the back
and make a crack.
The girls liked the hair,
liked the boy with the hair,
liked the boy with the leer,
liked the rocker.

In the locker
room every jock
with his pink rattail
comb and an ounce of swagger
camped in front of the mirror
for half an hour
after a shower,
the comb itself a weapon,
a rakish pocket dagger.

We wore our
Levi's low on our hips,
belt loops cut off
and the band folded over,
with white T-shirts and
a practiced glower.

Nobody told us how to be teenagers,
we figured it out on our own,
guided by hormones,
Dick Clark
and a firm belief in our
hair.

# The Old Professor Discovers the Sweet Egg of Discontent

A small boat moved across his line of sight,
one fisherman in the stern, one in the bow,
each holding a fishing rod.
They were working the weed line—as he had done
a hundred times—trolling so slowly
they seemed hardly to be moving at all,
so quiet, powered by an electric motor,
they seemed almost unreal, ethereal as a cloud.

"What contentment they must feel on this
perfect summer day," the old professor
said to himself, but then he recalled
what it felt like to be fishing—the restless
anticipation, the subtle discontent that
sat in the heart until, wham, a walleye
hit your bait, then the blood-rush of excitement
as you reeled it in and finally, perhaps, contentment,
but more likely an almost frenzied
hurry to get the fish in the well and your
line baited and into the water again. He
realized suddenly that contentment and fishing
had nothing to do with each other. "If it is
contentment they are after," he mused,
"I should tell them to reel in their lines and enjoy
this perfect summer day," but he had
hardly thought this when he realized
that *not* fishing in a barely moving boat on
a perfect summer day would only magnify their discontent.

The old professor smiled, remembering
Twain's famous observation about golf
being "a good walk spoiled," knowing
that for a golfer even a bad round is
better than a walk in a field
without a golf bag on the shoulder.

He sat in his chair sipping his drink,

watching a flock of ibis grazing on the lawn,
thinking how he might make a poem
about the men in the fishing boat.
He envied those slightly restless anglers
and realized that sitting there doing nothing
had not made him content and wondered
whether contentment was even possible — or desirable.
Suddenly he stood up with an "Aha!" and said,
"Discontent is more to be desired than contentment."

Pleased with his insight, he sat down and continued
the thought: "Contentment brings apathy and stasis but
discontent gives hope and hope ignites action.
When one ceases to hope — for a fish or a birdie
or the just-right metaphor to come along —
one's life becomes static, dull."

He paused for a moment then said,
"Discontent is the egg that hatches the bird of hope,"
smiled, muttered an apology to Miss Dickinson,
took up his pen and began to write:
"A small boat moved across his line of sight . . . ."

# Already and Not Yet

# January 29 — Already and Not Yet

Finally today, temperatures above freezing,
blue sky and a bright sun teasing me into
thoughts of spring. The edges of eaves
drip a steady chatter of happy gossip and the snow's
so white it almost blinds me. I could dance
were it not for the dark blue shadows of the ash trees that slash
across the frozen lawns to remind me that nothing is ever one thing.
The blue sky darkens, snow turns black, hoar frost grows on the gray walks,
then gradually the dark windows of houses flower, bright as marigolds.
This is what it is to live in a world straining to become
the Kingdom of God — a blue-white, January-thawed,
happy-sad, half-baked kingdom.

## February 7 — The Proper Way to Paint a Winter Morning

This morning the Lord himself went out among the trees of the town
and after brushing them with a coat of white enamel
took a bucket of paint from a different shelf
and topped off the taller trees in an iridescent magenta.
Of course the blackbirds thought it a dandy thing,
and the trees themselves gave him a hand,
but one school-marm angel, prim and proper,
who knows how things ought to be done,
grabbed a can of standard white and quickly slapped it
on the tops of the tall bright trees.

## March 26 — The Trees This Morning

each bare branch
flocked with frost
furred like a moose's rack
do not seem to realize that
they have been transformed
from black to white
from dead wood
to twisting spidery new life.
While they were sleeping
someone silently slipped these
white garments
over their shoulders and now
like little girls in brand new Easter frocks
they
don't
quite
dare
to
move.

## April 23 — Warm and Sunny

That chorus in the little
evergreen grove — you think
that's just sparrows and robins?
Open your ears and see:
the ruddy house finch, goldfinch,
blackbird, bonneted two-note chickadee.
Oh, and that brightness fluttering at the far end of the grove?
If you listen carefully there, you might
hear a hallelujah.

## May 4 — Nine Lines

A white line defines the road I ride.
Beside the road a green ditch butts against
Wire fence that severs ditch from fresh-plowed field.
Beyond those furrows, blue and black,
A flag of vibrant green, alfalfa field;
Behind the green a ragged stand of trees
And then a hazy ridge that slants southwest.
Horizon's next, and last a wispy line
Of cirrus draws my eye to heaven.

## June 20 — Mixed Messages

Instead of spending more time drinking coffee on the deck this morning,
flowers all around and the grass humming its cheerful little tune,
I strapped on my heavy backpack and biked toward this poem
which was sitting in my office computer waiting to be written.
Oh rare June day — no wind, sun a bright lemon in the heavens,
the streets swept clean, except for a squirrel smashed flat —
oh bright red blood — robins trilling their morning praise,
a paint crew chattering around my neighbor's house,
setting up ladders on the wheel chair ramp snaking
around the house, and further down the street,
a single blood-stained nightgown dancing
on the clothesline. Over it all the sky
so blue you could swim in it
forever and never reach
a shore.

## July 2 – A Grain of Seed Must Die

The Bloemendaal's lovely garden,
which flowered next to their garage,
painting long summer days with
poppies and phlox and daisies,
is gone,
plowed under and seeded over
with Kentucky bluegrass by the new owners.

The Bloemendaal's lovely garden,
which fragranced spring mornings
with peonies and iris,
and brightened late summer afternoons
with asters, bee balm and brown-eyed susans,
is gone,
plowed under and seeded over like old prairies
now filled with corn.

The seeds of the Bloemendaal's flowers,
asleep in the deep dark soil,
wait stolid and patient as saints,
for that day when the sky cracks open,
and the grass of the earth turns to fire.
Then soft rains will come, the seeds will
wake up,
and the Bloemendaal's garden again
will perfume the kingdom of God.

## August 23 — Return

Morning light leaks
ever so slowly
into the eastern sky
going from gray
to pale blue
to gradually brightening
shades of pink
and then
suddenly the sun
leaps up
like a beach ball that has been held beneath the water
Kaboom!
We are blinded
by the ball of light.

This is the way our Lord will return.
Suddenly
we will see him
after centuries of looking to the heavens
through fog or dust or dusk
or rose-colored glasses:
Immense, Bright, Undeniable.

## September 25 — Retired

This morning's walk was the same old walk past Tower Field,
the ash trees behind the left field fence
nearly bare now and the ground littered with yellow leaves,
wet and shiny after last night's rain. The horses
were the same two horses that have been grazing
in the green pasture for as long as I can remember,
a dun colored gelding and a bay stallion with a white
forehead blaze. They looked as if they were ready to go on parade,
their wet hides having been groomed all night by rain.
As I came up to where they stood in the southeast
corner of the field, they reached their heads over the wire fence
to smell me, so close my face touched the head of the bay.
Their nostrils were large and quivering
and their eyes full of dole.
I wondered what it was like to stand in a field for ten years
with nothing to do but graze and watch the seasons pass. I scratched
their noses briefly, murmured words of condolence, then bent
to push up the middle strand of fence wire and
climbed into the pasture.

## October 19 — Single-Heartedness

Not content with having spent all summer
pumping out giant crookneck squash,
some weighing more than seventeen pounds,
this old (in vegetable time) squash plant continues her work
as blithely and confidently as if it were early June instead of late October.
Wide green leaves flutter on the fence,
tiny squash curl fetus-like
under a sun-warmed green cocoon and
three bright yellow blossoms, full of purpose and ignorance,
grin into the late afternoon sun.
They do not know that the television soothsayers
have looked into their bird entrails and seen hoar frost
on tomorrow's lawns and death's wilt and shrivel
on every growing thing.

## November 20 – After the Harvest

The sharp, metallic whine of the fans drying
the corn in the immense concrete
bunker at the Co-Op Elevator
hangs in the mind like grief,
like mosquito whine,
an alarm clock buzzing in the next room.
It is never not there,
a gray noise like chronic backache
that takes its toll even when you are not aware of the pain,
the constant purr of the engine that runs our economy.

It arches its back over the entire town
and we gladly cuddle beneath it.

## December 12 — Winter

During the night
Old Smidt's garden
slipped on some
thin white pajamas
stitched with a fine design
of muskrat tracks,
leaned back into the earth
and fell asleep.

www.ingramcontent.com/pod-product-compliance
Lightning Source LLC
Chambersburg PA
CBHW032217040426
42449CB00005B/645